the Great Rounds Song-book

To the loving memory of my father,
Rubin Nelson, who sang his own
nameless melodies . . . .

the Great Rounds Song-book

BY ESTHER L. NELSON

ILLUSTRATIONS BY JOYCE BEHR

 Sterling Publishing Co., Inc.   New York

By the Same Author

Best Singing Games for Children of All Ages
Dancing Games for Children of All Ages
The Funny Songbook
Holiday Singing and Dancing Games
Movement Games for Children of All Ages
Musical Games for Children of All Ages
The Silly Songbook
Singing and Dancing Games for the Very Young

To many friends in many lands who have contributed freely their favorite rounds and helped to track down others: Clyde R. Appleton, Linda Babbitt, Judy Bronfman, Mary Cox, Joy Douglass, Pat Eisenberg, Dr. Joan Farber, Nancy Garniez, Davida Hirsch, Gundel Hoban, Johanna Holbeisen, Joy Hyman, Ruth Jacobson, Patricia McKernon, Helen Mintess, Jean Robotham, Risa Sokolsky, Fay Storch, Ted Warmbrand, Sol Weber, Roy Winyard who is the librarian at the Charing Cross Library in London, and Neura Yurberg.

And for the eighth time, a loving thanks to my very dear friend and editor, Sheila Barry, for her unending energy and confidence that it will all get done.

Library of Congress Cataloging in Publication Data
Main entry under title:

The Great rounds songbook.

Unacc. melodies; words in various languages.
Includes index.
Summary: An illustrated collection of 116 rounds from around the world, with lyrics, melody lines, background information, and instructions for singing.
1. Glees, catches, rounds, etc.—Juvenile. 2. Folk music. 3. Folk-songs. [1. Rounds (Music) 2. Folk songs.] I. Nelson, Esther L. II. Behr, Joyce, ill.
M1997.G816 1985   85-752326
ISBN 0-8069-4718-7
ISBN 0-8069-6234-8 (pbk.)
ISBN 0-8069-4719-5 (lib. bdg.)

Copyright © 1985 by Esther L. Nelson
Published by Sterling Publishing Co., Inc.
Two Park Avenue, New York, N.Y. 10016
Distributed in Australia by Capricorn Book Co. Pty. Ltd.
Unit 5C1 Lincoln St., Lane Cove, N.S.W. 2066
Distributed in the United Kingdom by Blandford Press
Link House, West Street, Poole, Dorset BH15, 1LL, England
Distributed in Canada by Oak Tree Press Ltd.
% Canadian Manda Group, P.O. Box 920, Station U
Toronto, Ontario, Canada M8Z 5P9
Manufactured in the United States of America
All rights reserved

CONTENTS

INTRODUCTION

Singing by yourself is fun. Singing with a group is even better. And singing with a group that sings rounds is the best of all! Why are rounds such fun to sing?

First of all, most of them are delightful songs—simple musically and easy to learn. They sound marvelous because you're making beautiful harmonies (without even trying!). You don't need any kind of musical accompaniment, so you can sing them anywhere—at school, at camp, on the bus, in the car, around the piano or the campfire. Everyone can (and will) take part: even the shyest person enjoys them, since no one has to be embarrassed about singing alone. Is it any wonder that rounds have been so popular for so long!

What is a round anyway? In 1863 Edward Rimbault said that defining a round is like "trying to define a circle without using your hands." But here's a start: A round is a short song of two or more lines or phrases. It is repeated by each singer—or group of singers—several times. The first singers complete a line or phrase before the second singers start, and because the phrases are of equal length, the two groups of voices harmonize. Rounds can have as few as two parts or many more (one of the rounds in this book can be sung with nine separate "voices"). All the voices are of equal importance, as in a fugue. The voices sometimes come together and sometimes separate, but they are almost always beautiful and interesting.

As the round starts with one voice (or group) singing, and then builds up to two or three or four or more, it ends in reverse, with each group dropping out as it finishes the round for the last time. The singing gradually diminishes until only one voice (or group) is left, and then none.

We run into the first mention of rounds in the 13th century, hundreds of years before the first one was actually published with music. Rounds were learned by ear and passed down from one generation to another in true oral folksong tradition. They were a popular form of indoor entertainment. In those days, of course, there was no chance of sitting and listening to the stereo or TV, so people made their own music, and the easiest way to do it was with their own voices. Their music told of their lives, their hopes, joys, sorrows—and what made them laugh—and it bound them together as they shared their emotions in song.

Sometimes rounds are called by other names. A "canon," for example, is a round, usually sung in three parts. A "catch" is a round, too. Popular in England in the 17th and 18th centuries, it was usually funny and bawdy, filled with double meanings, and it had something of a bad reputation. Other songs are sometimes confused with rounds. "Part songs," for example, are also sung in groups, but only one group sings the melody. Or the part song may consist of two or three altogether separate songs that—because of harmony and rhythm—"work" together. A "glee" is a part song for three or more voices that was especially popular in the 18th century, but it's not a round.

The songs in this book come from many sources and different countries. Some are serious (not too many!), some sad, some playful and some downright funny or silly. The topics cover a wide range of ideas, but they are all here because they have some particular charm, value or mood—some history, wit or charisma—of their own. Each and every one of them is a joy (though I admit I love some more dearly than others), because of its melody, its harmony, its message, its humor or its comments about life. The first round ever written down—"Summer Is A-Coming In"—is here, and so are some original rounds that have just been written and never appeared in print before. So the span of years covered by this book ranges from the 1200's to the present moment, when a new interest in rounds is surfacing all over the world. Rounds are playing a larger part in the repertoires of many singing groups. And some singers have begun to meet for the specific purpose of singing rounds together! A round has even been written about rounds:

When we sing rounds, we learn a great deal about music: we learn how to hold a tune alone and against another group that is singing the same melody at another time in space. We learn how to listen—how to recognize the harmonies, the different rhythmic patterns—one against the other—and the counterpoint.

The very first thing to do is to learn the song well. Sing it together in one group as many times as you need to really get to know it.

After that, divide the group into as many parts as you need. Though a song may show four parts, you can still sing it in only two parts, if you like. And it's a good idea to start out that way, in any case. Simply have the second group come in where it says ② in the music, or where it says ③. The sound will be very different, depending on which of these alternatives you choose. Try it both ways and see which one you like best.

Some of the rounds in this book use practically the same melody with different words. A song may be in a major key—and happy—but then it may appear in a minor key and undergo a complete character change—becoming haunting or sad or strange! Always keep the group aware of the quality of the music, the words and message, and sing the round accordingly.

Always sing softly, except when the song requires loudness for special effects. Round singing is a cooperative venture, and you need to be able to hear the other voices. Stay aware of them and how the sounds blend together.

When you sing without accompaniment, it's easy to go flat, so don't get discouraged if this happens at the beginning. As you learn to listen more to each other, think about the way the voices blend, and feel more comfortable about the whole thing, the flatness will improve.

If you like, you can decide beforehand how many times you want to sing each song through. But it may work better to choose one person who will make the decision as to when the round will end. Then all eyes must be glued on him or her for the signal to sing the song through for the last time.

Some groups enjoy the challenge of seeing how long they can go on singing a round. Others choose to sing a wider repertoire fewer times. Some groups choose to finish each song by singing in unison, instead of dropping the voice parts one by one. See which method your group prefers.

Many of us never experience the joy of being part of an orchestra and making music together with other people. That requires years of study of an instrument and not only being technically proficient, but also being able to read difficult orchestral arrangements. But we all have voices, and we can experience that same joy easily when we sing rounds—an activity that can only be enjoyed with other people. The pleasure and satisfaction is enormous! Try it— here are all my favorites!

FAMOUS FAVORITES

Row, Row, Row Your Boat

Row, row, row your boat,
Gently down the stream,
Merrily, merrily, merrily, merrily,
Life is but a dream.

This 19th Century song is probably one of the most famous rounds of all time.

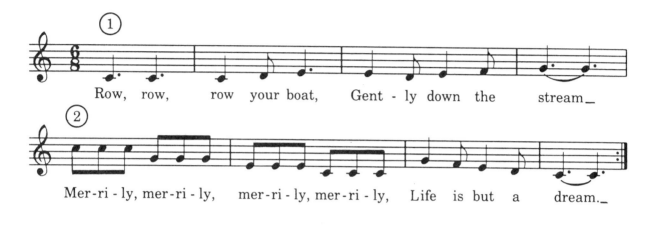

Row, row,   row your boat,   Gent - ly down the   stream_

Mer-ri - ly, mer-ri-ly,   mer-ri-ly, mer-ri-ly,   Life   is but a   dream._

Merrily We Roll Along

Merrily we roll along,
Roll along, roll along.
Merrily we roll along,
O'er the deep blue sea.

Mer - ri - ly   we   roll   a - long,   Roll   a - long,   roll   a - long,

Mer - ri - ly   we   roll   a - long,   O'er the deep blue   sea.

To the same tune: # Mary Had a Little Lamb

Mary had a little lamb,
Little lamb, little lamb,
Mary had a little lamb,
Its fleece was white as snow.

Three Blind Mice

Three blind mice, three blind mice,
See how they run, see how they run.
They all ran after the farmer's wife.
She cut off their tails with a carving knife.
Did you ever see such a sight in your life,
As three blind mice!

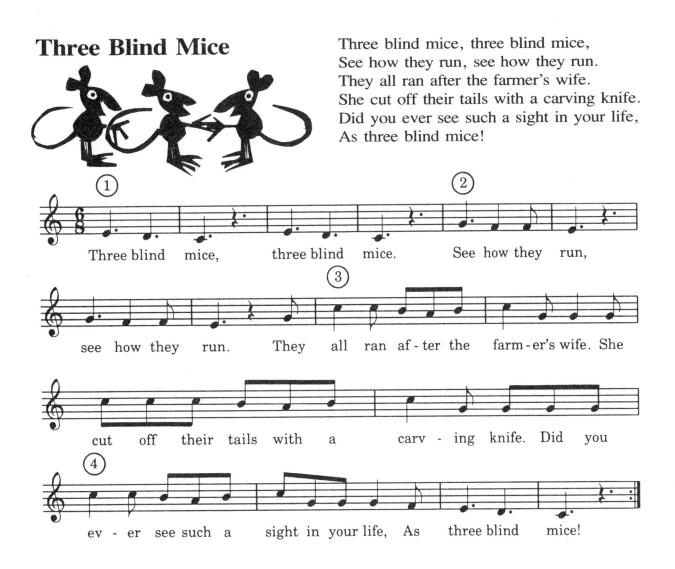

To the same tune: **The Healthy Round**

Wheat germ, herbal tea,
Yogurt, Vitamin C.
I'm eating my dinner organic'ly,
Al*fal*fa sprouts and salt from the sea,
I top it all off with sesame
And wheat germ. . . .

Frère Jacques

Frère Jacques, Frère Jacques,
Dormez-vous, dormez-vous?
Sonnez les matines,
Sonnez les matines,
Ding, dong, dong.
Ding, dong, dong.

which means:

Are you sleeping, are you sleeping,
Brother John, Brother John?
Morning bells are ringing,
Morning bells are ringing,
Ding, dong, dong.
Ding, dong, dong.

Of course, everyone knows "Frère Jacques," but do you know "Martinello" or "Fray Felipe" (Brother Philip)? Both versions are Spanish, and they're both fun to sing. And also to this tune—try "If the Cat," which is a real surprise!

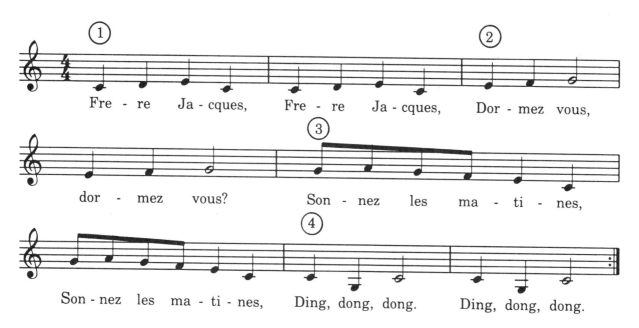

To the same tune:

Martinello

Martinello, Martinello,
¿Quieres tú, quieres tú?
Toca la campana, toca la campana,
Din, din, don.
Din, din, don.

Fray Felipe

Fray Felipe, Fray Felipe,
¿Duermes tú, duermes tú?
Tocan las campanas, tocan las campanas,
Tan, tan, tan.
Tan, tan, tan.

If the Cat

If the cat, if the cat
Washes her face—or her ear—
'Tis a sign the weather will be fine,
Fine and clear, fine and clear.

White Coral Bells

White coral bells, upon a slender stalk,
Lilies of the valley deck your garden walk.
Oh, how I wish that I could hear them ring.
That will happen only when the fairies sing.

This classic round is pitched high to capture the quality of the delicate flowers it describes. If coral bells could actually ring, they'd sound like this.

Apple Trees in Bloom

Sweet the evening air of May,
Soft my cheek caressing.
Sweet the unseen lilac spray,
With its scented blessing.

White and ghostly in the gloom,
Shine the apple trees in bloom,
Apple trees in bloom!
Apple trees in bloom!

Come Follow

Come follow, follow, follow,
Follow, follow, follow me.
Whither shall I follow, follow, follow—
Whither shall I follow—follow thee?
To the greenwood, to the greenwood,
To the greenwood, greenwood tree.

This beautiful old English song was written by John Hilton (1599–1657).

① Come fol - low, fol - low, fol - low, Fol - low, fol - low, fol - low me.

② Whith-er shall I fol-low, fol-low, fol-low— Whith-er shall I fol-low—fol-low thee?

③ To the green-wood, to the green-wood, To the green-wood, green-wood tree.

FOOLING AROUND

WITH SOUND

FROG SONGS

Here are two jumping-frog songs, and they're both delightful to sing. Take your pick— or go from one to the other.

Song of the Frogs

Hear the lively song of the frogs in yonder pond.
Crick, crick, crickity-crick—Brrr-ump!

Hear the live - ly song Of the frogs in yon - der pond.

Crick, crick, crick - i - ty-crick– Brr - ump!

Hear the Frogs

Hear the frogs! Plop! Plop!
There they go! Plop! Plop!
Why don't they stop?
Plop! Plop!

Hear the frogs! Plop! Plop! There they go! Plop! Plop! Why don't they stop? Plop! Plop!

Softly Sings the Donkey

Softly sings the donkey
At the break of day.
If you do not feed him,
You will hear him say:
Hee-haw! Hee-haw! Hee-haw! Hee-haw! Hee-haw!
Hee-haw! Hee-haw! Hee-haw! Hee-haw! Hee-haw!

Softly sings the donkey
As he goes to grass.
He can sing no better,
'Cause he is an ass.
Hee-haw! Hee-haw! Hee-haw! Hee-haw! Hee-haw!
Hee-haw! Hee-haw! Hee-haw! Hee-haw! Hee-haw!

The first half of this melody sounds like the tune of "The Eensy Beensy Spider Went up the Water Spout," but then it changes. It's fun to try different voices when you sing "Hee-haw," from a high falsetto to a basso profundo!

Sweetly the Swan Sings

Sweetly the swan sings:
Do di ah do,
Do di ah do,
Do di ah do.

This simple, delicate round is extremely beautiful in its harmonies.

Sweet-ly the swan sings: Do di ah do, Do di ah do, Do di ah do.

The Swan Sings

The swan sings:
Teer-i-li-o,
Teer-i-li-o,
Teer-i-li-o.

In this version of "Sweetly the Swan Sings," the melody is almost the same, but the rhythm and the words are different.

The swan sings, Teer-i - li - o, Teer-i - li - o, Teer-i - li - o.

Canoe Round

My paddle's keen and bright,
Flashing with silver,
Follow the wild goose flight,
Dip, dip and swing.

Dip, dip and swing her back,
Flashing with silver,
Follow the wild goose track,
Dip, dip and swing.

Soft and in a minor key, this round was written by Margaret Embers McGee in 1918. You can feel the canoe gliding noiselessly through the water as you sing it.

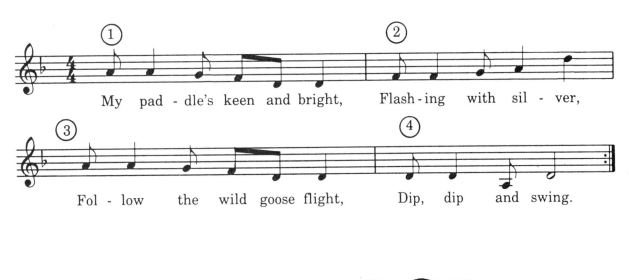

My pad - dle's keen and bright, Flash-ing with sil - ver,
Fol - low the wild goose flight, Dip, dip and swing.

The Wind in the Willows

The wind in the willows—
Sighing like a solitary soul alone.

Take a deep breath just before "sighing like a solitary soul alone," because the rhythm is very fast and the words need to be sung clearly. It actually *feels* like the wind blowing through the trees, as you sing. The faster you do this round, the more difficult it is; it's easy when you sing it slowly.

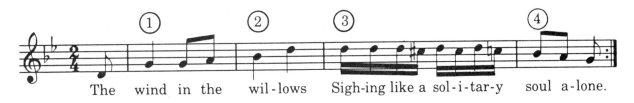

The wind in the wil - lows Sigh-ing like a sol-i-tar-y soul a-lone.

Clocks

Hear the steeple clock go tick-tock, tick-tock,
Little mantel clock goes tick-tock, tick-tock,
 tick-tock, tick-tock,
Now the little pocket watch goes tick-a-tock-a,
 tick-a-tock-a, tick-a-tock-a, tick.

With only four notes, this song has lots of rhythmic variety. It goes back and forth from half notes to quarter notes and then ends with quick eighth notes. Sing it solemnly and slowly, like a somber clock in a church steeple.

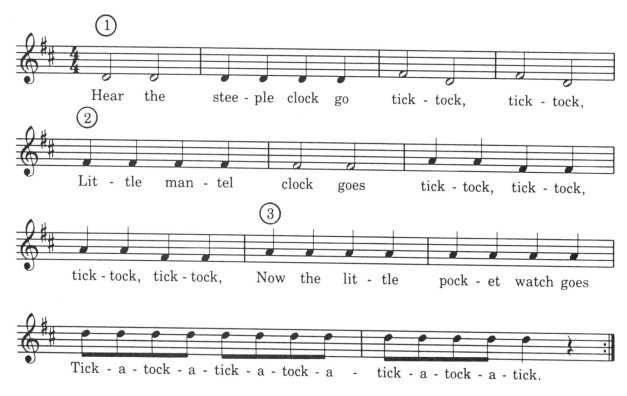

And Yet Another Great Tumba Round

Tumba, tumba, tumba, tumba,
Tumba, tumba, tumba!
Tumba, tumba, tumba, tumba,
Tumba, tumba, tumba!

Tra-la-la, la-la-la-la-la,
La-la-la-la-la-la,
Tra-la-la, la-la-la-la-la,
La-la-la-la-la-la!

Tra-la-la-la-la,
La-la-la-la-la,
La-la-la-la-la-la!
Tra-la-la-la-la,
La-la-la-la-la,
La-la-la-la-la-la!

In this exciting tumba round, the rhythm really grabs you! With three sections going at the same time, hold onto your hat—and your seat!

Derry Ding Ding Dason

Derry ding ding dason,
I am John Cheston,
We wee-don, we wo-den,
We wee-don, we wo-den,
Bim boom, bim boom,
Bim boom, bim boom.

In this old English round about a weaver, you can hear the sound the shuttle makes as it flies back and forth over the loom.

GREAT OLDIES

Goose Round

Why shouldn't my goose
Sing as well as thy goose,
When I paid for my goose
Twice as much as thou?

This old English nonsense round is easy to sing, and it's an excellent icebreaker—a good song to start with. Sing it with great seriousness!

① Why should-n't my goose ② Sing as well as thy goose,

③ When I paid for my goose ④ Twice as much as thou?

Laugh, Ha-Ha!

Laugh, ha-ha!
Here's a merry jest,
But if you will laugh last,
You will laugh best.

① Laugh, ha, ha! ② Here's a mer-ry jest, ③ But if you will

④ laugh last, You will laugh best!

Hey-Ho, Nobody Home!

Hey-ho, nobody home,
Meat nor drink nor
Money have I none,
Yet will I be mer-ry—

With its mediaeval sound, this hearty song in a minor mode, is one of the best-loved rounds.

To the same tune: Vent Frais (Cool Wind)

This lovely round comes from France.

Vent frais, vent du matin,
Sous le vent le sommeil des montagnes.
Jolie du vent qui passe—
Allons dans le grand. . . .*which means:*

Cool wind, wind of the morn,
Under the wind the sleeping mountains lie.
Joyous wind that blows—
Let's run in the great. . . .

Scotland's Burning

Scotland's burning,
Scotland's burning,
Look yonder,
Look yonder!
Fire, fire, fire, fire,
But we have no water!

We've come across two versions of this round. In the other one, London is burning.

STREET SONGS

These rounds date back to the days when merchants sang of their wares, telling of the quality of the merchandise and the price.

Chairs to Mend

Chairs to mend, old chairs to mend,
Mackerel, fresh mackerel,
Any old rags, any old rags?

Chairs to mend, old chairs to mend Mack - er - el, fresh
mack - er - el, An - y old rags? an - y old rags?

Cherries So Ripe

Cherries so ripe and so round,
The best in the market found,
Only a penny a pound.
Who will buy?

Cher - ries so ripe and so round, The best in the mar - ket
found, On - ly a pen - ny a pound. Who will buy?

34

STREET SONGS

Bento-Uri

	which means:	
Oyako domburi!		Folks—here's the menu!
Osushi bento		Box lunch—fish
Sandowitchee!		Sandwiches!
Lamuneni!		Soda!
Saida!		Cider!
Gyunyu! (sounds like "goo-noo")		Milk!

This street vendor's call is heard at Japanese railroad stations as trains arrive. Bento means "box lunch," and "osushi" is raw fish.

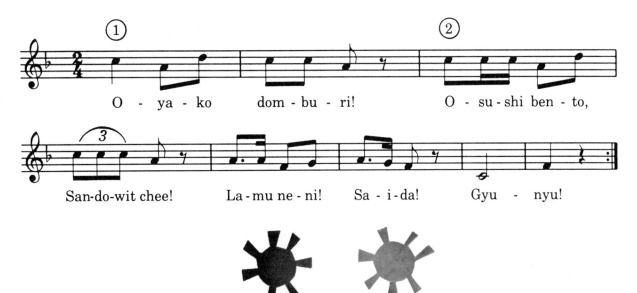

O - ya - ko   dom - bu - ri!   O - su - shi ben - to,

San-do-wit chee!   La - mu ne - ni!   Sa - i-da!   Gyu - nyu!

White Sands and Grey Sands

White sands and grey sands.
Who'll buy my white sands?
Who'll buy my grey sands?

In the 18th Century—before blotters were invented—sand was sprinkled over a freshly written page to dry the ink. The sand was then returned to a small container to be saved and used again. White to begin with, it gradually became grey with use. The sand sellers would buy back the grey sand and resell it at bargain prices to those who couldn't afford the luxury of pure white sand.

White sands and grey sands. Who'll buy my white sands? Who'll buy my grey sands?

The Little Bell at Westminster

The little bell at Westminster
Goes "Ding, dong, ding-a-dong."

The simplest of all the bell rounds, this song is about one of the bells of the British houses of Parliament, which rings every hour.

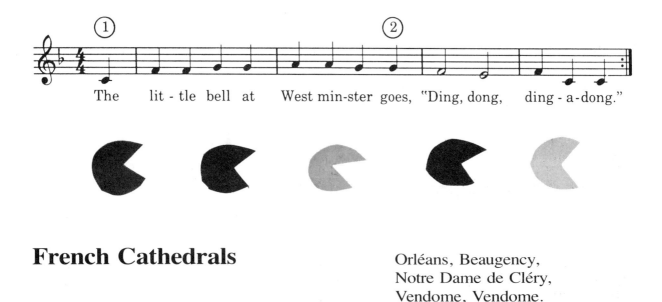

The lit-tle bell at West-min-ster goes, "Ding, dong, ding-a-dong."

French Cathedrals

Orléans, Beaugency,
Notre Dame de Cléry,
Vendome, Vendome.

This solemn French round can also be sung twice as fast and in 6 parts, each group coming in after two measures. The names in the first verse are those of famous French cathedrals. The second verse was written in 1717, evidently by someone who felt sympathy for the monotonous task of the church bells.

Or-le-ans, Beau-gen-cy, No-tre Da-me de Cle-ry, Ven-do-me, Ven-do-me.

Quel chagrin,
Quel ennui,
De chanter toute la nuit
Les heures, les heures.

which means:

What a nuisance,
What a bore,
Counting, counting all night
The hours, the hours.

36

Ding Dong Bell

Ding dong, ding dong, ding dong bell,
Ding dong bell, ding dong bell,
Ding dong, ding dong bell!
Hark the merry, merry bells,
They ring a ding dong bell.

Another old English bell round, this song has great variety. It starts with a slow, steady beat, gets faster and builds to an increasing, uneven rhythm and rich fullness of sound.

Great Tom Is Cast

Great Tom is cast
And Christ Church bells ring:
One, two, three, four, five, six,
And Tom is last.

Written by Oxford Dean Henry Aldrich in the late 1600s, this round celebrates the bell "Great Tom," which hangs in Oxford's Christ Church in the tower built by Sir Christopher Wren. If you're in Oxford at 9 o'clock any night, you can hear it ring the curfew (there are 101 strokes). The ⁀ symbol is called a *fermata*, and it tells you to hold the note a little longer than you normally would. All three parts reach the fermata at the same time, which makes for a lovely, resonant sound. A challenge to sing, the music spans a wide range (an octave and a half!) from high to very low.

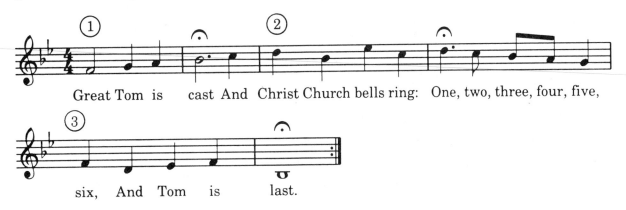

Where Is John?

Where is John?
The old grey hen has left her pen,
Oh, where is John?
The cows are in the corn again,
Oh, John!

Based on a melody written by the Czechoslovakian composer, Frederick Smetana (1824–1884), this captivating round is especially good to sing when you're annoyed with people for being late, for not being there when you want them, or for not getting things done. It makes you laugh at yourself and feel better. It's also fun to sing if you're in a good mood!

Where is John? The old grey hen has left her pen, Oh,

where is John? The cows are in the corn a-gain, oh,

John!

Little Tom Tinker
Got burned by a clinker
And he began to cry,
"Ma! Ma!
What a poor fellow am I!"

Little Tom Tinker

You can sing this simple round in as many parts as you choose—2, 4 or 8. If you do it in two parts, start the second part at ⑤. If you do it in four parts, start the second part at ③. (A clinker is the ash from a fire.)

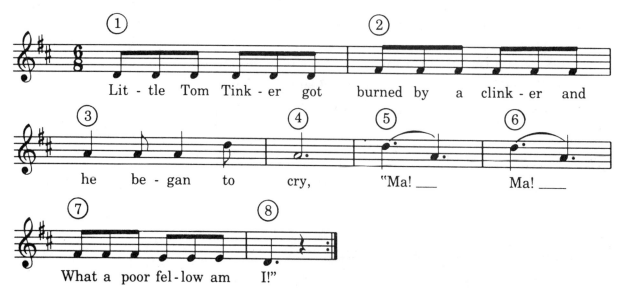

Lit-tle Tom Tink-er got burned by a clink-er and

he be-gan to cry, "Ma! __ Ma! __

What a poor fel-low am I!"

Ride a Cock Horse

Ride a cock horse to Banbury Cross,
To see a fine lady upon a white horse.
Rings on her fingers and bells on her toes,
She shall have music wherever she goes.

With its rhythmic changes and odd melody line, this old English round is difficult but extremely interesting. It is also written in five parts, which is unusual.

Ride a cock horse to Ban-bur-y Cross, To see a fine la-dy up-on a white horse. Rings on her fin-gers and bells on her toes, She shall have mu-sic where ev-er she goes.

Now All the Woods
Are Waking

Now all the woods are waking,
The sun is riding high.
Wake up now, get up now,
Before the dew is dry!

You can sing this little round in as many as 8 parts or as few as 2; take your choice. Or perhaps you'd like to try all of them (one at a time!). If you want to sing it in two parts, come in on ④. If you want to sing it in four parts, have the second part come in on ③, the third come in on ⑤, and the last come in on ⑦.

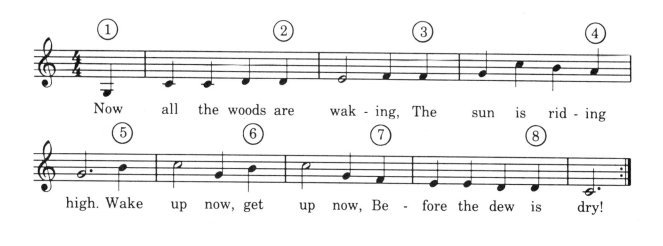

Now all the woods are wak - ing, The sun is rid - ing high. Wake up now, get up now, Be - fore the dew is dry!

The Hart He Loves
the High Wood

The hart, he loves the high wood,
The hare, he loves the hill.
The knight, he loves the bright sword,
The lady loves her will.

Another period piece, this English round was composed in 1680.

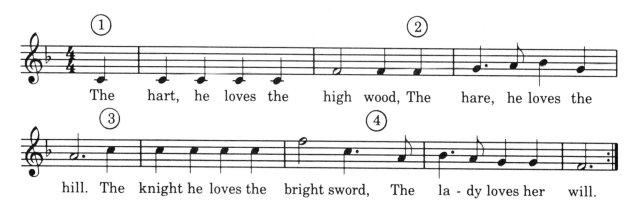

The hart, he loves the high wood, The hare, he loves the hill. The knight he loves the bright sword, The la - dy loves her will.

Summer Is A-Coming In

Summer is a-coming in, loudly sing cuckoo.
Groweth seed and bloweth mead
And springs the wood anew. Sing, cuckoo!
Ewe bleateth after lamb,
Low'th after calf the cow,

Bullock starteth, buck too verteth.
Merry sing, cuckoo,
Cuckoo, cuckoo!
We'll sing'st thou, cuckoo!
Oh, cease thou never now!

This very famous English round, the earliest one we know of, comes from a 13th Century manuscript. It was set to music three centuries later by Palestrina, the Italian composer of church music. A "bullock" is a steer. "Starteth" means to give a start or to jump. "Verteth" means to stroll or gambol.

Tallis Canon

All praise to thee my God this night
For all the blessings of the light.
Keep me, oh, keep me, Lord of life,
Within thy love and free from strife.

This round is a period piece! The music was written by Thomas Tallis in the 16th Century, and the words were added by Thomas Kenn in 1695. You'll find another round by Thomas Tallis on page 52.

All praise to thee my God this night For all the bless-ings of the light. Keep me, oh keep me, Lord of life, With- in thy love and free from strife.

FUNNY ROUNDS

Thirty Purple Birds

Plain:
Thirty purple birds,
Sitting on the curb,
A-chirping and a-burping
And a-eating dirty worms.

Toidy-toid Street version:
Toidy poiple boids,
Sitt'n on the coib,
A-choipin' and a-boipin'
And a-eatin' doity woims.

This silly song originated in New York, and it's fun to perform whether you sing it plain or with a New York accent (the "Toidy-toid Street" version).

Thir - ty pur - ple birds, sit - ting on the curb, A -
chirp-ing and a - burp-ing And a - eat - ing dirt - y worms.

To Stop the Train

To stop the train in cases of emergency,
Pull on the chain! Pull on the chain!
Penalty for improper use: Five pounds.

This English round is based on a notice posted in a railway car.

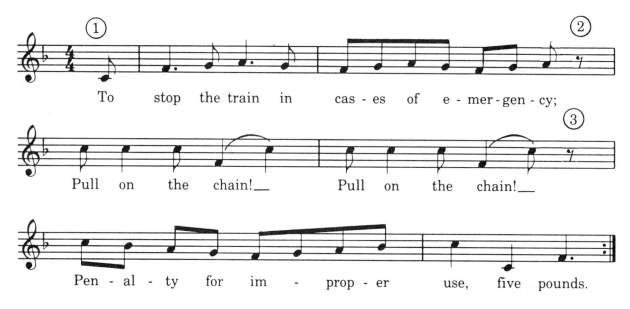

To stop the train in cas - es of e - mer - gen - cy;
Pull on the chain!__ Pull on the chain!__
Pen - al - ty for im - prop - er use, five pounds.

Grasshoppers Three

Grasshoppers three a-fiddling went,
Hey-ho, never be still.
They paid no money toward their rent,
But all day long with elbow bent,
They fiddled a tune called rillaby, rillaby,
Fiddled a tune called rillaby rill.

This spirited round has a unique quality and moves at a fast pace.

I Don't Care for Underwear

I don't care for underwear,
I just use underroos.
I don't care for underwear,
I just use underroos.

I don't care for un-der-wear, I just use __ un - der - roos, __

I don't care for un-der-wear, I just use__ un - der-roos.

To the same tune: **Sur le Pont d'Avignon**

Sur le pont d'Avignon,
L'on y danse, l'on y danse,
Sur le pont d'Avignon,
L'on y danse tout en rond!

which means:

On the bridge of Avignon,
They are dancing, they are dancing,
On the bridge of Avignon,
They are dancing in a circle.

That's right—the tune for "I Don't Care for Underwear" is actually "Sur le Pont d'Avignon," the old French song that celebrates the bridge at Avignon. You can also do this round as a dance, with ladies and gentlemen bowing graciously to each other.

Black Socks

Black socks, they never get dirty.
The longer you wear them, the stronger they get.
Sometimes I think I should launder them,
Something keeps telling me,
"Don't wash them yet—not yet—not yet!"

This song is everybody's favorite!

Black socks, they nev-er get dirt-y. The long-er you wear them, the

strong-er they get. Some-times I think I should laun-der them.

Some thing keeps tell-ing me, "Don't wash them yet— not yet— not yet!"

To ope their trunks
The trees are never seen.
How did they then
Put on their robes of green?
They leave them out.

To Ope Their Trunks

To ope their trunks The trees are nev-er seen. How

do they then put on their robes of green? They leave them out.

Sandy McNab

There was an old fellow named Sandy McNab,
Who had for his supper a very fine crab,
And had to be carried home in a cab.

This round comes from 19th Century Scotland.

There was an old fel - low named San - dy Mc - Nab, Who

had for his sup - per a ver - y fine crab, And

had to be car - ried home in a cab.

Mister Bach

Mister Bach wrote sev'ral tunes
Just like this—
Organ sonatas, fugues, cantatas—
I never know which is which!

This rollicking round is based on Bach's famous "Little Fugue in G Minor."

Mis - ter Bach wrote sev' - ral tunes_ Just like this.

Or - gan son - a - tas, fugues, can - ta - tas, I ne - ver know which is which!

My Dame Hath a Lame Tame Crane

My Dame hath a lame tame crane.
My Dame hath a crane that is lame.
Good, gentle Jane, let my Dame's tame crane
Feed and come home again.

Written by Matthew White in 1630, or thereabouts, this great round is a tongue twister!

My Dame hath a lame tame crane. My Dame hath a crane that is

lame. Good, gen-tle Jane, let my Dame's lame tame crane

Feed and come home_ a - gain.

Benjy Met a Bear

Benjy met a bear.
The bear met Benjy.
The bear was bulgy.
The bulge was Benjy.

① Ben - jy met a bear.__ The bear met Ben - jy. The
③ bear was bul - gy. The bulge was Ben - jy.__

50

A Ram Sam Sam

A ram sam sam,
A ram sam sam,
Guli, guli, guli, guli, guli,
Ram sam sam.
A ram sam sam,
A ram sam sam,
Guli, guli, guli, guli, guli,
Ram sam sam.

A ra-fi, a ra-fi,
Guli, guli, guli, guli, guli,
Ram sam sam.
A ra-fi, a ra-fi,
Guli, guli, guli, guli, guli,
Ram sam sam.

This two-part Moroccan round is spirited, and the words are wonderful to say.

The Baby Lima Bean Song

Oh, how I wish that I could be
A baby lima or a pea,
Sitting in my little pod
With my green and shiny bod.

Oh, how I wish that I could be A ba - by li - ma or____ a____ pea, Sit - ting in my lit - tle pod With my green and shin - y____ bod.

Here Lie the Bones

Here lie the bones of lazy Fred,
Who wasted precious time in bed.
Some plaster fell upon his head,
And, Lord be praised, our Freddie's dead.

The words to this round were adapted from a 19th Century tombstone. The music was written by Thomas Tallis (1510-1585), who has been called the father of English cathedral music. Another Tallis round appears on page 42.

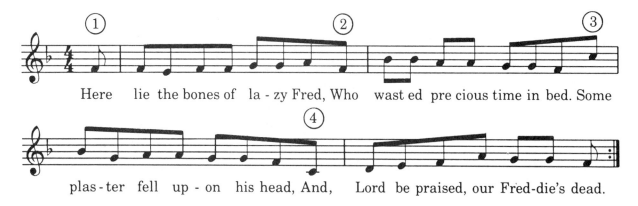

Here lie the bones of la - zy Fred, Who wast ed pre cious time in bed. Some plas - ter fell up - on his head, And, Lord be praised, our Fred-die's dead.

Poor Tom

Have you seen the ghost of Tom?
Long white bones with the skin all gone—
Poor Tom!
Wouldn't it be chilly with no skin on!

This spooky round is especially appropriate for singing around the campfire or the fireplace or on Halloween.

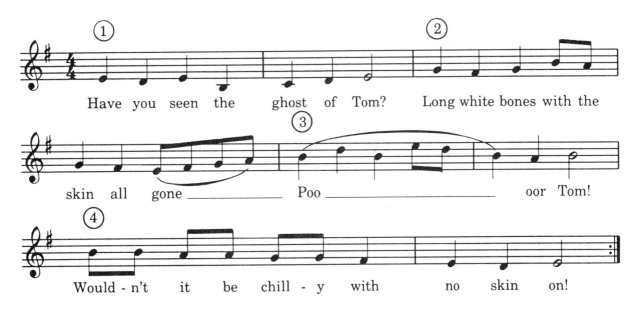

Have you seen the ghost of Tom? Long white bones with the

skin all gone _____ Poo _____ oor Tom!

Would - n't it be chill - y with no skin on!

Mister Rabbit

Mister Rabbit, Mister Rabbit,
Your ears are mighty long.
    Yes, my Lord, they're put on wrong!
Ev'ry little soul must shine, shine, shine,
Ev'ry little soul must shine, shine, shine.

Mister Rabbit, Mister Rabbit,
Your foot is mighty red,
    Yes, my Lord, I'm almost dead!
Ev'ry little soul must shine, shine, shine,
Ev'ry little soul must shine, shine, shine.

Mister Rabbit, Mister Rabbit,
Your coat is mighty grey.
    Yes, my Lord, 'twas made that way!
Ev'ry little soul must shine, shine, shine,
Ev'ry little soul must shine, shine, shine.

Mister Rabbit, Mister Rabbit,
Your tail is mighty white.
    Yes, my Lord, and I'm gettin' out of sight!
Ev'ry little soul must shine, shine, shine,
Ev'ry little soul must shine, shine, shine.

This Afro-American song can be sung in 9 parts, which makes it very busy and lots of fun. It also has many stanzas, which is unusual in a round and makes singing time very long.

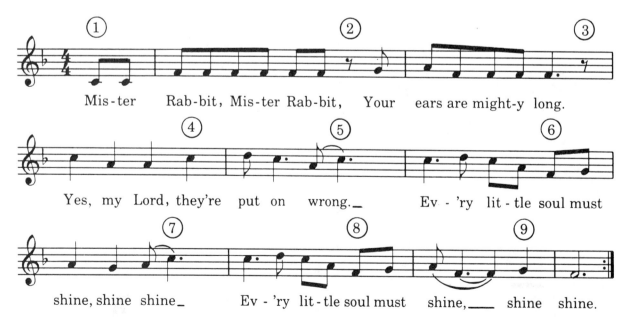

54

Let Simon's Beard Alone

Let Simon's beard alone, alone,
Let Simon's beard alone.
'Tis no disgrace to Simon's face,
For he had never one.
Then mock not, nor scoff not,
Nor leer not, nor sneer not,
But rather him bemoan.

Written by John Hilton in the 17th Century, this fascinating round is hard to sing, with its minor mode, its length, and its unfamiliar melody. The second and third parts are extremely difficult, but worth the effort!

Let Si-mon's beard a - lone, a-lone, Let__ Si-mon's beard a-

lone.__ 'Tis no dis - grace to Si - mon's face, For__

he had nev - er one.__ Then mock not, nor scoff not, Nor

leer not, nor sneer not, But rath - er him be - moan.__

I'm Not Strong, Sir!

I'm not strong, sir,
Sure, 'tis wrong, sir,
Such high notes my voice do strain.
I can't sing a note, sir,
Something hurts my throat, sir,
Though I try my best,
'Tis all in vain.
I'm quite hoarse, sir,
So, of course, sir,
I cannot sing this round again!

This hilarious Victorian round is practically impossible to sing! Its range goes from low B to high D (an octave and a half). Sing it once, if you can!

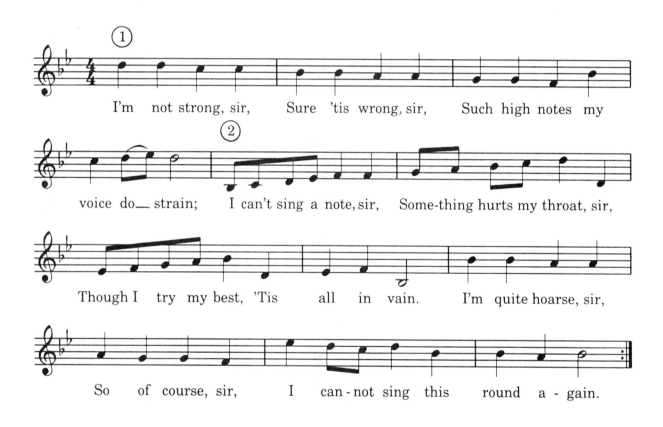

I'm not strong, sir, Sure 'tis wrong, sir, Such high notes my

voice do— strain; I can't sing a note, sir, Some-thing hurts my throat, sir,

Though I try my best, 'Tis all in vain. I'm quite hoarse, sir,

So of course, sir, I can-not sing this round a-gain.

GETTING
THE MESSAGE

Early to Bed

Early to bed and early to rise,
Makes a man healthy and wealthy and wise—
Wise, healthy and wealthy.

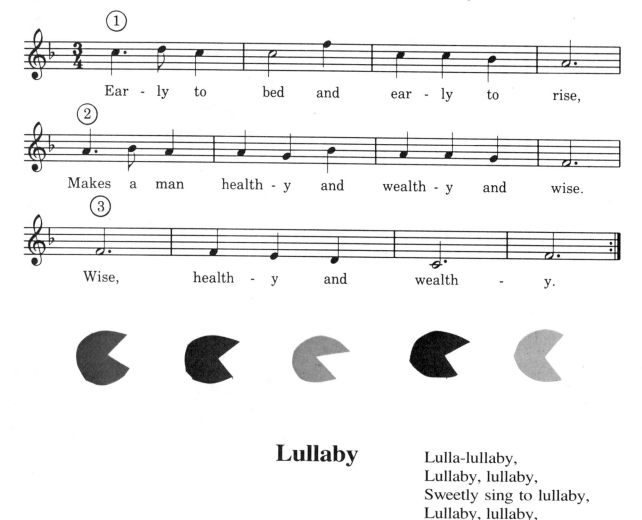

Lullaby

Lulla-lullaby,
Lullaby, lullaby,
Sweetly sing to lullaby,
Lullaby, lullaby,
Sweetly sing to lullaby.

This lullaby has a simple melody, but you need a simple melody if you're going to have 9 parts singing at the same time! You can sing it in any number of parts you want, though, starting with 2.

Man's Life's a Vapor

Man's life's a vapor full of woes.
He cuts a caper, down he goes.
Down he, down he, down he, down he,
Down he goes.

This 4-line exercise in negative thinking is delightful to sing.

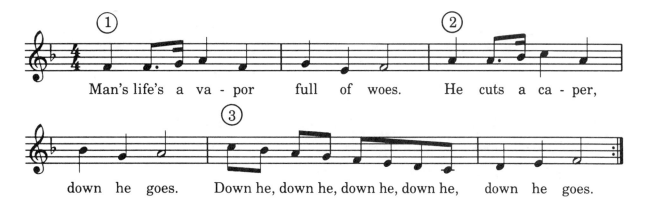

Man's life's a va - por   full   of woes.   He cuts a ca - per,

down he goes.   Down he, down he, down he, down he,   down he goes.

Let Us Endeavor

Let us endeavor
To show that whenever
We join in a song
We can keep time together.

This easy round is terrific to sing when you've just botched up a more difficult one.

Sing, Sing Together

Sing, sing together, merrily, merrily sing.
Sing, sing together, merrily, merrily sing.
Sing, sing, sing, sing.

The words are simple, the melody is simple (all on a major chord), and singing this round gives you a warm, uplifted feeling.

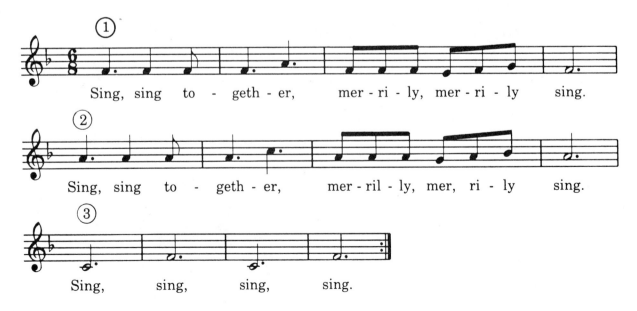

Music Alone
Shall Live

Though all things perish
From under the sky,
Music alone shall live,
Music alone shall live,
Music alone shall live,
Never to die.

In German:

Himmel und Erde
Mussen vergehn.
Aber die Musici,
Aber die Musici,
Aber die Musici,
Bleiben bestehn.

This beautiful German round reflects the feelings of us all.

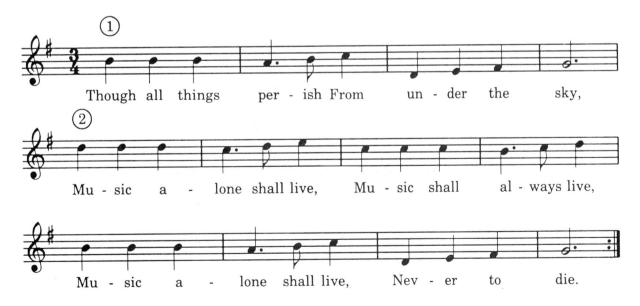

① Though all things per - ish From un - der the sky,

② Mu - sic a - lone shall live, Mu - sic shall al - ways live,

Mu - sic a - lone shall live, Nev - er to die.

Veggie Round

Grains and beans
To balance proteins
And seeds and greens
And a dairy down down.

This charming round, written by Ted Warmbrand from Tucson, Arizona, tells you one way to eat a balanced diet.

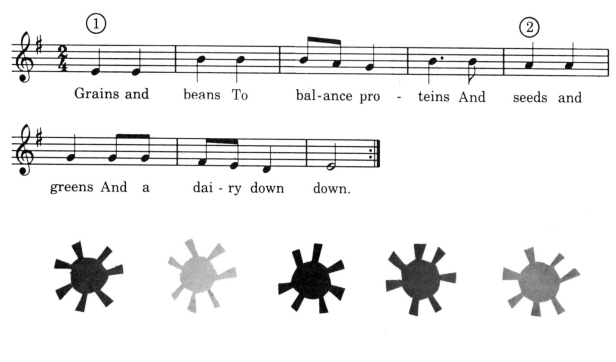

Grains and beans To bal-ance pro - teins And seeds and

greens And a dai - ry down down.

Artichokes and Broccoli

Artichokes and broccoli,
Lettuce and tomatoes,
Brussels sprouts and celery,
Onions and potatoes.

Written by Professor Clyde Appleton, who teaches at the University of North Carolina in Charlotte, this vegetable shopping list has a quaint 19th Century sound.

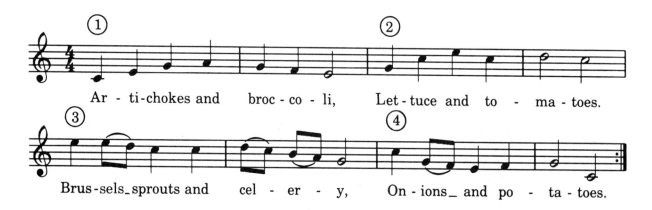

Ar - ti-chokes and broc - co - li, Let - tuce and to - ma - toes.

Brus-sels sprouts and cel - er - y, On - ions and po - ta - toes.

Avocado Round

I've got an avocado in my 12-string case
And an E-string in my shoe.
There's a blind, purple people-eater in my bed.
Now what am I to do?

Fun to sing but not so easy, this unusual round is a hit with everyone, young and old.
We've even heard about a nursery-school group that was enchanted by it!

The Singing School

I will sing you a song of the old
  Singing School
And the sounds you there may hear,
Of the do, re, mi and the A, B, C,
And the voices ringing clear.

Sing the song with accent strong,
Loud and clear the tone prolong:
Do, re, mi, fa, sol, la, ti, do.
'Tis the scale of C, you know.
Common, double, triple measures, too,
Are among the many things we do.

This delightful old round is long and difficult, but it teaches rhythm, tone quality and solfeggio (do-re-mi!).

Kin and Kith

We would be in less danger
From the wiles of a stranger,
If our own kin and kith
Were more fun to be with!

Odd-sounding, mediaeval in feeling, this haunting round is written in the minor mode. You'll like it more each time you sing it.

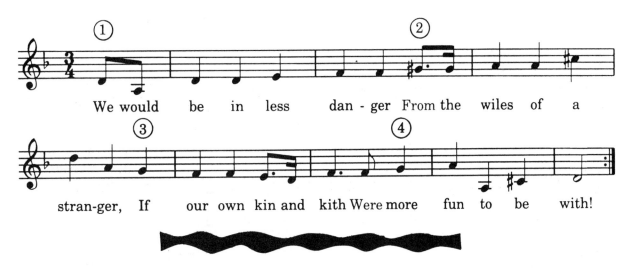

We would be in less dan-ger From the wiles of a stran-ger, If our own kin and kith Were more fun to be with!

C-O-F-F-E-E

C-O-F-F-E-E, don't drink so much coffee.
Not for children is this Turkish drink,
Keeps you nervous, pale and out of sync.
Don't let caffeine stew make a robot
  out of you!

In German:

C-A-F-F-E-E, trink nicht so viel Caffee.
Nicht für Kinder ist der Türkentrank;
Schwächt die Nerven, macht dich blass
  und krank,
Sei doch kein Muselmann, der ihn nicht ·
  las-sen kann.

This helpful round comes from Germany.

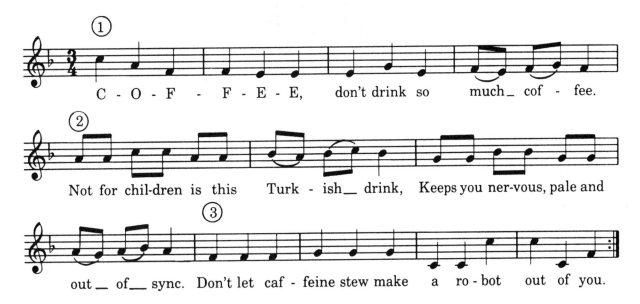

C - O - F - F - E - E, don't drink so much_ cof - fee.
Not for chil-dren is this Turk - ish_ drink, Keeps you ner-vous, pale and
out _ of_ sync. Don't let caf - feine stew make a ro - bot out of you.

Thirty Days Hath September

Thirty days hath September,
April, June and November.
All the rest have thirty-one,
Saving February alone,
Which has twenty-eight,
Rain or shine,
And on leap year twenty-nine.

Thir - ty days hath Sep - tem - ber, A - pril, June and No -
vem - ber. All the rest have thir - ty - one, Sav - ing
Feb - ru - a - ry a - lone, Which has twen - ty - eight, rain or
shine, And on leap year twen - ty - nine.

SILLY ROUNDS

Donkeys and Carrots

Donkeys are in love with carrots,
Carrots aren't in love at all.
Hee-haw, hee-haw,
That's a crazy, funny call.

In French:

Les anes aim' les carrottes,
Les carrottes n'aim' pas les anes.
Hee-haw, hee-haw,
C'est idiot, mais c'est marrant.

This silly round comes from Belgium.

① Don-keys are in love with car-rots, ② Car-rots aren't in love at all. ③ Hee-haw, hee-haw, ④ Lis-ten to that sil-ly call.

You can zip any names you like into this round. For example:

Harold is in love with pancakes,
Pancakes aren't in love at all,
Hee-haw, hee-haw,
That's a crazy, funny call.

Chickens
Get into the Tomatoes

The chickens get into the tomatoes.
The chickens get into the tomatoes.
Even the rabbits inhibit their habits
When carrots are green.
Even the rabbits inhibit their habits
When carrots are green.

This terrific round is meant to be spoken instead of sung. You can sing it in a monotone, if you want, using just one note, as shown here.

① The chick-ens get in-to the to-ma-toes,

The chick-ens get in-to the to-ma-toes.

② Ev-en the rab-bits in-hib-it their hab-its when

car-rots are green.

One Bottle Pop

One bottle pop,
Two bottle pop,
Three bottle pop,
Four bottle pop,
Five bottle pop,
Six bottle pop,
Seven bottle bottle pop.

Fish and chips and vinegar,
Vinegar, vinegar,
Fish and chips and vinegar,
Pepper, pepper, pepper salt.

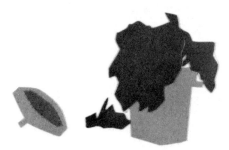

Don't throw your trash in my back yard,
My back yard, my back yard,
Don't throw your trash in my back yard,
My back yard's full!

The three separate stanzas of this round are unrelated to each other, but they work beautifully together.

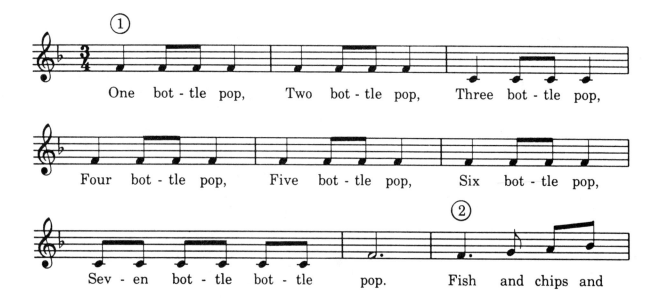

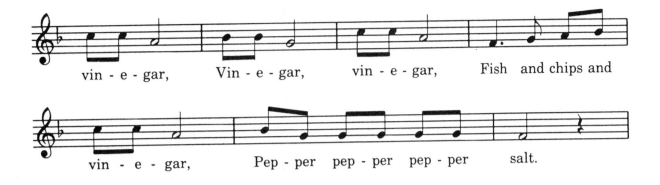

vin - e - gar,   Vin - e - gar,   vin - e - gar,   Fish   and chips and

vin - e - gar,   Pep - per   pep - per   pep - per   salt.

③

Don't throw your trash in   my back yard,   my back yard,   my back yard,

Don't throw your trash in   my back yard,   my back yard's   full!

I Want a Chocolate Malted

I want,
I want a malted,
I want a chocolate malted,
I want a chocolate malted.

The music for this round comes from Bach's "Toccata in G Minor." It is based on the Grand Fugue, and the combination of that music and these words is thirst-quenching!

Reuben, Reuben

Reuben, Reuben, I've been thinking,
What the heck have you been drinking?
Looks like water, tastes like wine—
Oh, my gosh, it's turpentine!

On Mules We Find

On mules we find
Two legs behind
And two we find before.

We stand behind
Before we find
What the two behind be for.

When we're behind
The two behind,
We find what they be for.

So stand before
The two behind,
Behind the two before.

This absurd round is sung to the tune of "Auld Lang Syne."

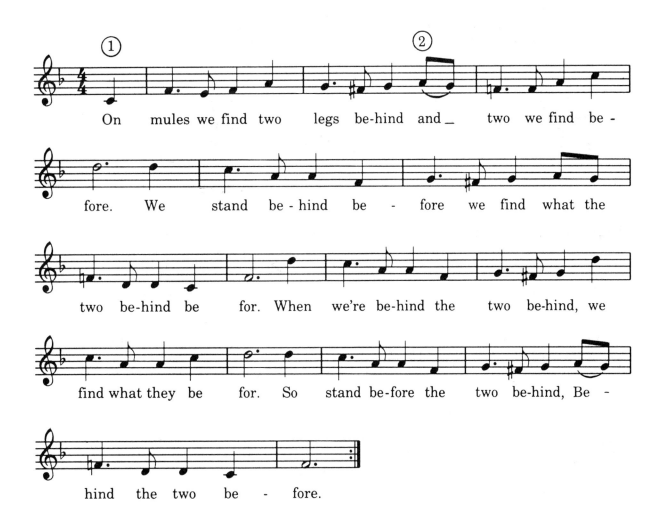

On mules we find two legs be-hind and _ two we find be-fore. We stand be-hind be - fore we find what the two be-hind be for. When we're be-hind the two be-hind, we find what they be for. So stand be-fore the two be-hind, Be - hind the two be - fore.

Eating Is Fun

Eating is fun,
Yum, yum, yum, yum,
Basting and tasting
Will never be done.

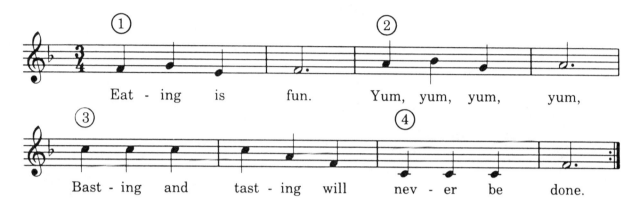

Eat - ing   is   fun.   Yum, yum, yum, yum,

Bast - ing and tast - ing will nev - er be done.

You can zip any activity you like into this round. For example:

Hiking is fun,
One, two, three, four,
Camping and tramping
Will never be done.

or:

Talking is fun,
Yak, yak, yak, yak,
Ratting and chatting
Will never be done.

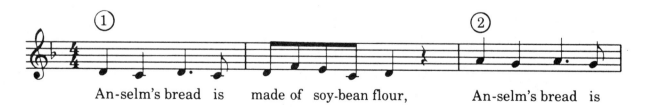

Anselm's Bread

Anselm's bread is made of soybean flour,
Anselm's bread is made of soybean flour.
You could use white instead
But there's nothing like that soybean bread.

It sounds old, but this round was written fairly recently. You can sing it in 4 parts or in 7, each new part coming in at the start of a new measure.

An-selm's bread is   made of soy-bean flour,   An-selm's bread is

made of soy - bean flour. You could use white in - stead, But there's

noth - ing like that soy - bean bread.

The Duchess at Tea

I sat next to the Duchess at tea.
It was just as I thought it would be.
Her rumblings abdominal were simply phenomenal,
Everyone thought it was me!

Try singing this 4-part round stiffly, with total seriousness!

I sat next to the Duch-ess at tea. __ It was just as I

thought it would be. __ Her rum - bl - ings ab - dom - in - al were

sim - pl - y phen-om - en - al, Eve-ry-one thought_ it was me!

The Dangers of Knowing Your Name

There once was an ichthyosaurus
Who lived when the earth was all porous.
But he fainted with shame
When he first heard his name
And departed a long time before us.

This original round by Patricia McKernon is based on an old limerick.

There once was an ich - thy - o - saur - us   Who

lived when the earth was all   por - ous.   But   he

faint - ed   with shame when he   first heard his name And de -

part - ed   a   long   time   be - fore   us.

The Old Woman from Pride

There was an old woman from Pride
Ate too many apples and died.
The apples, fermented inside the lamented,
Made cider inside her inside.

The music to this adaptation of the classic limerick was provided by Sol Weber, a folk collector with the Pineswood Folk Club.

Can You Dig That Crazy Gibberish?

Can you dig that crazy gibberish?
Can you dig it?
Can you dig it?
Can you dig that crazy gibberish?
Can you dig it?
Can you dig it?
Oh, look there's a chicken comin' down the road.
Oh, look there's another one sittin' on the fence.
Ma-a! Ma-a!
Get that whatsamagig off my tractor!

This is a speaking round—said or sung all on one note—so rather than melody, it is the play of rhythm against rhythm that makes it so exciting.

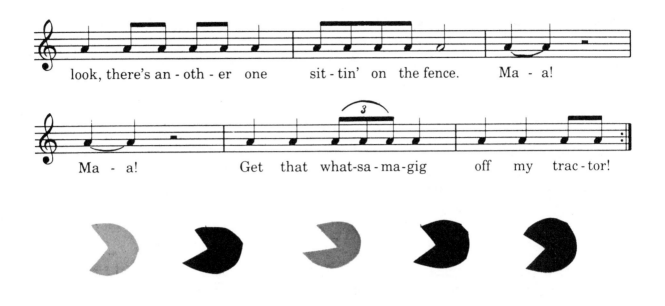

look, there's an - oth - er one sit - tin' on the fence. Ma - a!

Ma - a! Get that what-sa - ma-gig off my trac - tor!

A Man with a Wry Nose

Peter White will never go right,
Would you know the reason why?
Would you know the reason why?
He follows his nose wherever it goes,
And that stands all awry, awry,
And that stands all awry!

This difficult English round was composed by Richard Brown around 1735.

Pe - ter White will nev - er go right, Would you

know_ the rea - son why?_ Would you know_ the rea - son

why?_ He fol - lows his nose wher - ev - er it goes, And

that stands all a - wry,_ a-wry, And that stands all a - wry._

Sweet Potato Round

When sweet potatoes cook,
How good, how good,
How good they smell, yum, yum.
Especially when seasoned well,
Yum, yum, yum, yum, yum, yum, yum, yum.

This super-syncopated round really catches you and carries you along. How *few* times can you get away with singing it? It's like eating sweet potato chips—impossible to stop after just one! Try it with maracas!

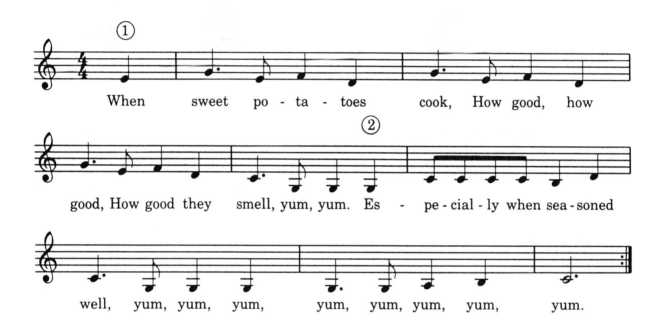

When sweet po - ta - toes cook, How good, how

good, How good they smell, yum, yum. Es - pe - cial - ly when sea - soned

well, yum, yum, yum, yum, yum, yum, yum, yum.

Alleluia

Alleluia, alleluia!
Alleluia, alleluia!

Al - le - lu - ia,   al - le - lu - ia!   Al - le - lu - ia,   al - le - lu - ia!

Glad and Good

Glad och gud skall Mänskan vara
Hela livet intill döden.

which sounds like:

Glah-d oak gude skah mahn-sahn vah-ra
He-illa leave-it in-till derd-an.

and means:

Happy and good should man be
All his life until he dies.

This simple, catchy round is a great favorite in Sweden.

Glad och gud skall   Män-skan va - ra   Hee - la - li - vet   In - still dö - den.

In the German version, the meaning is different:

which means:

Froh zu sein, bedarf Mann wenig
Und wer froh ist, der ist Konig.

It doesn't cost much to be happy,
And if you're happy, you're a king.

Join in Singing Hallelujah

Join in singing Hallelujah!
Hallelujah! Amen—
Amen—Hallelujah!
Hallelujah! Amen.

This round uses only four notes in different patterns, so it's particularly easy to sing—and satisfying.

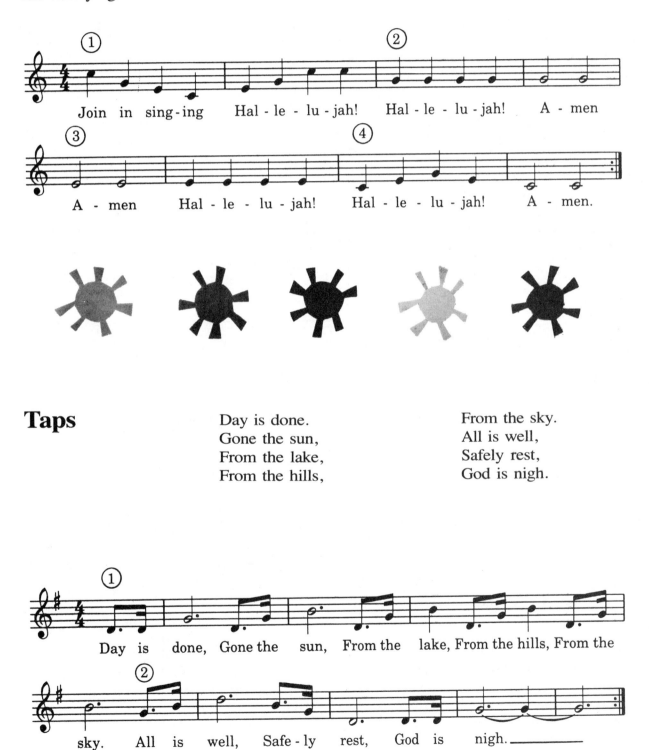

① Join in sing-ing Hal - le - lu - jah! ② Hal - le - lu - jah! A - men
③ A - men Hal - le - lu - jah! ④ Hal - le - lu - jah! A - men.

Taps

Day is done.
Gone the sun,
From the lake,
From the hills,

From the sky.
All is well,
Safely rest,
God is nigh.

① Day is done, Gone the sun, From the lake, From the hills, From the
② sky. All is well, Safe - ly rest, God is nigh._____

The More We Get Together

The more we get together, together, together,
The more we get together, the happier we'll be.
For your friends are my friends
And my friends are your friends.
The more we get together, the happier we'll be.

The_ more we get to - geth-er, to - geth-er, to - geth-er, The_

more we get to - geth - er, the hap - pier we'll be. For

your friends are my friends And my friends are your friends. The_

more we get to - geth - er, the hap - pier we'll be.

To the same tune: **Ach Du Lieber Augustin**

This happy-sounding round is actually one of the most popular of the German nursery rhymes. It's interesting, though, that many German children's songs combine happy melodies with grim words. This song tells of Augustin (St. Augustine, some say, or an order of monks in Germany during the Middle Ages), who fell victim to the plague but survived. It goes like this:

Ach du lieber Augustin, Augustin, Augustin,
Ach du lieber Augustin, alles ist hin.
Geld ist weg, gut ist weg,
Augustin liegt im dreck,
Ach du lieber Augustin, alles ist hin.

Pronunciation Guide:
Augustin: Ow-gus-teen
Lieber: leeb-er
Alles: ah-lus
Weg: veck
Liegt: leeked

which means:

Oh, my darling Augustin, Augustin, Augustin,
Oh, my darling Augustin, everything is lost.
Money is gone, home is gone,
Augustin is lying in the dirt,
Oh, my darling Augustin, everything is lost.

Make New Friends

Make new friends
But keep the old—
One is silver
And the other gold.

Make new friends, But keep___ the___ old___

One is sil - ver and the oth - er gold.

To the same tune:

Ah, Poor Bird

This haunting English round can be sung in either 2 or 4 parts. If you want to sing it in 2 parts, start the second part on ③.

Ah, poor bird,
Take your flight
Far above the sorrows
Of this sad night.

Ah, poor bird,
Mourn the tree
Where sweetly thou did'st warble
In thy wanderings free.

To the same tune:

Lasagna

Lasagna,
Baked ziti,
Pasta fazoola,
We love thee!

You can do this round in 2 parts or in 4, as shown here. If you want to do it in 2 parts, start the second part at ③.

Ego Sum Pauper

Ego sum pauper.
Nihil habeo.
Cor meum dabo.

pronounced:

Ee-go sum paw-per.
Nih-hill hah-bay-oh.
Kaw may-um dah-boh.

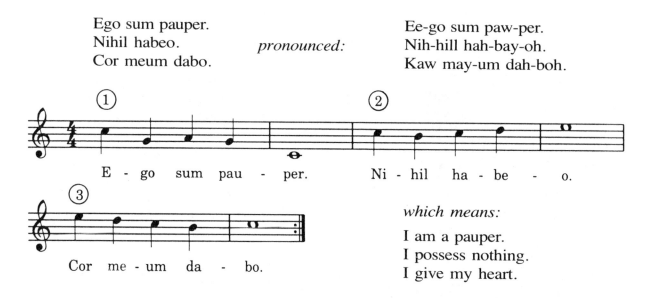

which means:

I am a pauper.
I possess nothing.
I give my heart.

This Latin round is simple in its words, its melody and its message.

Dear Friends

Dear friends, dear friends,
Let me tell you how I feel.
You have given me such riches,
I love you so!

The first line of this song sounds like "Hey-Ho, Nobody Home," but the quality of it is totally different. "Hey-Ho" has a hearty, robust feeling, and this song is haunting.

Christmas Is Coming

Christmas is coming,
The geese are getting fat.
Please to put a penny in the old man's hat.
Please to put a penny in the old man's hat.

If you haven't got a penny,
A ha'penny will do,
And if you haven't got a ha'penny,
Then God bless you!

This charming three-part round was originally a nursery rhyme. Written by F. Nesbitt, it was first published in England in the 17th Century.

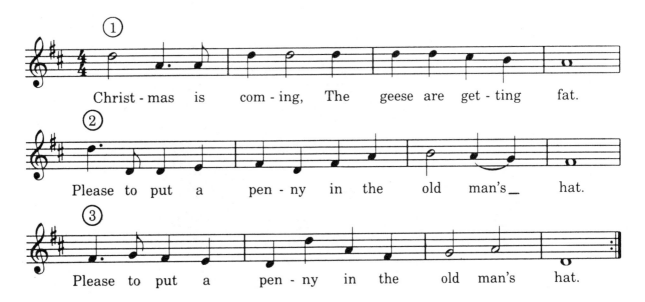

Shalom Chaverim

Shalom, which means "peace," has other meanings as well. You can use it to say "hello" or "good-bye." In this moving Hebrew song, it means both "peace" and "good-bye."

Shalom chaverim,
Shalom chaverim,
Shalom, shalom,
L'hit ra-ot, l'hit ra-ot,
Shalom, shalom.

which means:

Good-bye (or peace), my friend,
Good-bye, my friend.
Good-bye, good-bye.
Till we meet again, till we meet again,
Good-bye, good-bye.

Pronunciation Guide:

shalom—shah-lome
chaverim—hah*-vah-rim
l'hit—lay-hit
ra-ot—rah-utt

Another version:

Glad tidings we bring of peace on earth,
Good will towards men,
Of peace on earth, of peace on earth,
Good will towards men.

*actually like the "ch" sound in the German word "na*ch*t."

Haida, Haida

Haida, haida, haida-da, haida,
Haida, haida, haida.
Haida, haida, haida-da, haida,
Haida, haida, haida.

Haida, haida-da,
Haida, haida, haida, haida.

Haida, haida-da,
Haida, haida, haida, haida.

Haida, haida-da, haida, haida,
Haida, haida.
Haida, haida-da, haida, haida,
Haida, haida.

This round is a "nigun," a song created by the Jewish people of Eastern Europe. It has no actual words. Sometimes, when you sing it fast, it sounds like: "High-da, high-da, high-diddy-DYE-da," which gives it an earthy gypsy quality.

Dona Nobis Pacem

Dona nobis pacem, pacem.
Dona nobis pacem.
Dona nobis pacem.
Dona nobis pacem.
Dona nobis pacem.
Dona nobis pacem.

This beautiful round in three parts was composed by Palestrina in the 16th Century. It means "Give us peace."

Do - na no - bis pa - cem, pa - cem, Do - na __

no - bis pa - cem. Do - na no - bis

pa - cem, Do - na no - bis pa - cem. Do - na

no - bis __ pa - cem, do - na no - bis pa - cem.

pronounced: Doe-nah no-biss pah-chem.

Vegetable Grace

Thank you for this food,
This food, this glorious, glorious food!
And the animals and the vegetables
And the minerals that made it possible.

Written by Patricia McKernon, this song is also a prayer of thanksgiving.

Thank you for this food, This__ food, this glo - ri - ous, glo - ri - ous

food!   And the   an - i-mals   and the   vege - ta-bles   And the

min-er-als__ that made it   pos - si-ble!

Happy Days

Happy days to all those that we love!
Happy days to all those that love us!
Happy days to all those that love them

That love those   That love those
That love them   That love us.

It's hard to keep this round straight, but the thoughts are good.

Hap - py   days   to   all   those   that   we   love!__ Hap - py

days   to   all   those   that   love   us!_____ Hap - py

days   to   all   those   that   love   them That love those   that   love

them That love those   that   love   us. _____

We're on the Homeward Trail

We're on the homeward trail,
We're on the homeward trail,
Singing, singing, ev'rybody singing,
As we go.

We're on the homeward trail,
We're on the homeward trail,
Singing, singing, ev'rybody singing,
Homeward bound.

You can sing this very lovely, lyrical round when you're coming back from anything, anywhere. The beautiful harmonies make it difficult to stop singing.

We're on the home-ward trail, We're on the home-ward trail. Sing-ing, sing-ing, ev-'ry bod-y sing-ing As we go. We're on the home-ward trail, We're on the home-ward trail, Sing-ing, sing-ing, ev-'ry bod-y sing-ing, Home-ward bound!

Evening Bells

Shadows of evening fall o'er the town.
Now tolls the bell, the evening bell.
Soon the people will all be sleeping.
All's well, all's well.

This lovely round was written by Clyde R. Appleton. Sing it softly and lyrically.

Shad - ows of eve - ning fall o'er the town. Now tolls_ the bell, the eve - ning bell. Soon the peo - ple will all ___ be sleep - ing. All's well, all's well.

Good Night to You All

Good night to you all,
And sweet be your sleep.
May silence surround you,
Your slumber be deep.
Good night, good night,
Good night, good night.

Good night to you all and sweet be your sleep; May si - lence sur - round you, your slum - ber be deep. Good night, good night, Good night, good night.

93

INDEX OF FIRST LINES

INDEX

About the Author:

Esther L. Nelson, M.A., Dance Education, is one of the foremost educators in music and dance for children. She is the originator, with composer Bruce Haack, of the highly acclaimed "Dance, Sing and Listen" records and other music and dance participation recordings produced by her record company, Dimension 5. These records, the books she has written about music and movement and her much loved songbooks have already become classics and are used in schools, libraries and homes throughout the English-speaking world. Listed in *Who's Who of American Women* as well as *The World Who's Who of Women*, she conducts classes and workshops at colleges and educational conferences throughout the world to help teachers use movement and music to enhance the learning process.